# Collins Primary Maths
# Pupil Book 2

Series Editor: Peter Clarke

Authors: Andrew Edmondson, Elizabeth Jurgensen,
Jeanette Mumford, Sandra Roberts

# Contents

| | | |
|---|---|---|
| Counting and properties of numbers | To count on in steps of 3 from any small number to at least 50, then back again | 31, 32 |
| | To count on in steps of 3, 4 or 5 from any small number to at least 50 then back again | 33 |
| Reasoning about numbers | To recognise simple patterns and relationships | 34, 35 |
| Problems involving "real life" | To solve word problems involving numbers in "real life" | 39 |
| Understanding multiplication and division | To understand division as grouping | 40, 42 |
| | To recognise that division is the inverse of multiplication | 40, 42 |
| Rapid recall of multiplication and division facts | To derive quickly division facts corresponding to the 2, 5 and 10 times tables | 41 |
| Problems involving "real life" and money | To solve word problems involving numbers in "real life" | 43 |
| Rapid recall of multiplication and division facts | To derive quickly doubles of 5 to 100 and 50 to 500 and the corresponding halves | 44 |
| Mental calculation strategies (x and ÷) | To use doubling or halving, starting from known facts | 45 |
| Fractions | To begin to recognise simple equivalent fractions: for example, five tenths and one half, five fifths and one whole | 46, 47, 48, 49, 50, 51, 52, 53, 54,55 |
| Organising and using data | To solve a given problem by organising and interpreting numerical data in simple lists, tables and graphs, for example, bar charts | 56, 57, 58, 59, 60, 61, 62, 63, 64 |

## Acknowledgements

The publisher would like to thank the following for their valuable comments and advice when trialling and reviewing Collins Primary Maths 3 materials.

Concetta Cino – Barrow Hill Junior School, London
Mrs B Crank – Heron Hill County Primary, Kendal, Cumbria
Elizabeth Fairhead – Puttenham C of E School, Guildford, Surrey
Mrs D Kelley – Green Lane First School, Bradford
Alison Lowe – Goddard Park Primary School, Swindon
Sarah Nower – Watchetts Junior School, Camberley, Surrey
Miss M Richards – Birchfield Primary School, Birmingham
Mrs S Simco – Heron Hill County Primary, Kendal, Cumbria
Janice Turk – Sacred Heart Junior School, London
Chris Wilson – Woodville School, Leatherhead, Surrey

● Read and begin to write the vocabulary of comparing and ordering numbers, including ordinal numbers to at least 100
● Compare two given three-digit numbers, say which is more or less

Sp 1, 1

# Fruit card ordering

## Refresher

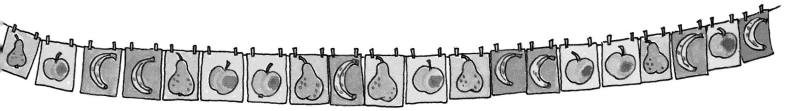

1 Write down the name of the fruit in these positions.

   a 3rd _banana_    b 1st         c ninth          d 7th
   e tenth           f 13th        g twentieth      h 18th

2 Write the positions of the pears.

## Practice

Work in pairs.

A B C D E F G H I J K L M N O P Q R S T U V W X Y Z
1st   3rd                                       20th

1 Write down a three- or four-letter word without letting your partner see. Then write down the position of each letter. Show each other your position numbers and find your partner's word. Write three more words. Now send your partner a short message.

Your word is CAT.

2 Deal 30 three-digit cards between you. Together, put one card on the table. The person with the higher card wins both cards. Play until no cards are left. The player with the most cards is the winner.

# Rabbit rounding up

## Refresher

1 How far has each rabbit travelled? Write your answer to the nearest 10 metres.

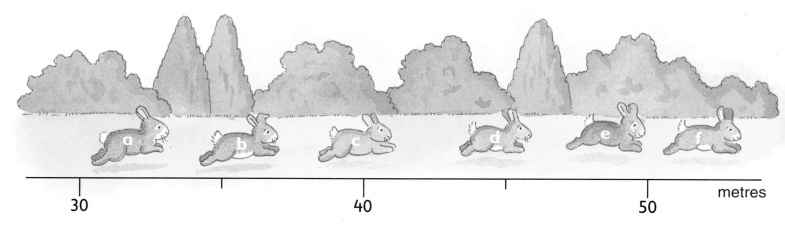

30        40        50        metres

## Practice

1 Round the lengths to the nearest 10 metres.

a          b          c          d          e

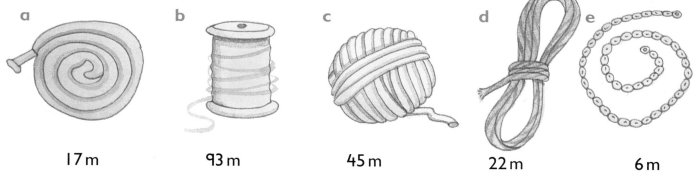

17 m       93 m       45 m       22 m       6 m

2 Round the distances to the nearest 10 metres.

a          b          c          d          e

Beach      Park       Library    Museum     Toilets
35 m       53 m       18 m       96 m       5 m

# Weight estimation

## Refresher

1 Write down the weight of these items.

a

b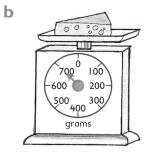

c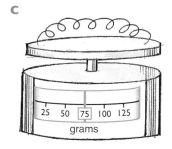

d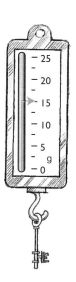

2 Write your estimate of the weight of these items.

a

b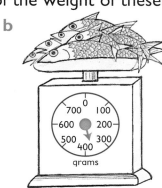

c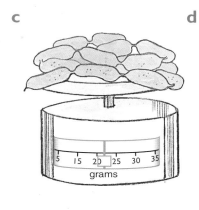

d

## Practice

1 Write down the weight of these items.

a

b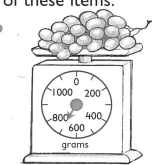

c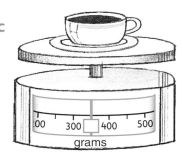

d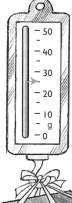

2 Write your estimate of the weight of these items.

a

b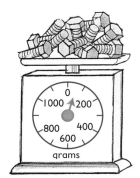

c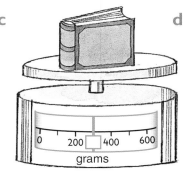

d

# Fish food numbers

Each fish can eat two pieces of food at a time.
The numbers on the food, when added or
subtracted, must equal the number on the fish.

**Example**

7 + 4 = 11

## Refresher

1  Work out four meals for each fish.

## Practice

1  Work out five meals for each fish.

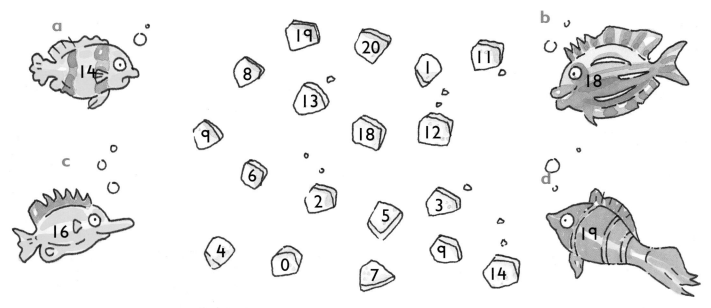

8

# Number line race game

## Refresher

### Race to 6

A game for two players     You will need:

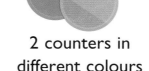

2 counters in different colours

A 1–6 die

### How to play:

- Place your counter on one of the "start" positions.
- Decide who will be moving from 1 to 6 and from 12 to 6.
- Take turns to throw the die and move that number of spaces in your direction.
- Before moving the counter on, say the number you are on, for example, 4. Add or find the difference.
- The winner is the first person to reach 6.
- Now swap directions and play again.

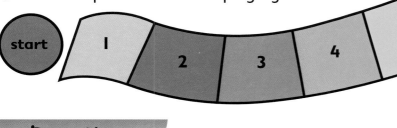

## Practice

### Race to 10

A game for two players     You will need:

2 counters in different colours

A 0–9 die

### How to play:

- Place your counter on the "start" position.
- Decide who will be moving from 1 to 10 and from 20 to 10.
- Take turns to throw the die and move that number of spaces in your direction.
- The winner is the first person to reach 10.
- Now swap directions and play again.

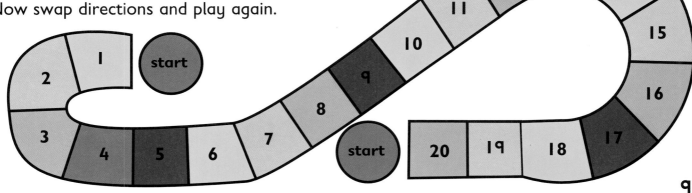

9

# Paper chain calculations

## Refresher

Hold the answers in your head

1 Add these three numbers together.

a 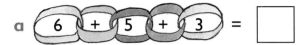 6 + 5 + 3 = ☐    b 4 + 7 + 2 = ☐

c 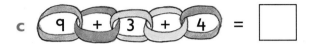 9 + 3 + 4 = ☐    d 5 + 3 + 6 = ☐

e 7 + 2 + 1 = ☐    f 4 + 6 + 3 = ☐

g 6 + 3 + 7 = ☐    h 5 + 4 + 7 = ☐

i 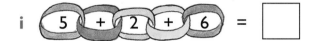 5 + 2 + 6 = ☐    j 1 + 6 + 4 = ☐

## Practice

1 Add these four numbers together.

a 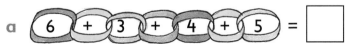 6 + 3 + 4 + 5 = ☐    b 9 + 2 + 5 + 1 = ☐

c  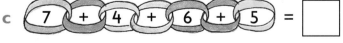 7 + 4 + 6 + 5 = ☐    d 8 + 3 + 6 + 2 = ☐

e 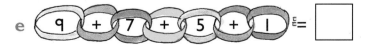 9 + 7 + 5 + 1 = ☐    f 6 + 9 + 7 + 3 = ☐

g 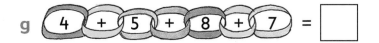 4 + 5 + 8 + 7 = ☐    h 6 + 8 + 7 + 2 = ☐

i 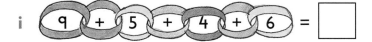 9 + 5 + 4 + 6 = ☐    j 9 + 8 + 7 + 6 = ☐

# Calculation bricks

## Refresher

I  Use the numbers on the bricks to build an addition calculation. Think about the order to use.

a

b

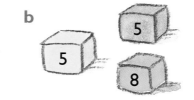

c

11 + 7 + 3 = 21

d

e

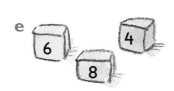

f

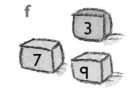

g

h

i

## Practice

I  Use the numbers on the bricks to build an addition calculation.

a

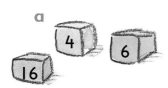

b

c

d

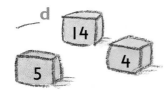

e

f

g

h

i

# Fruity addition

## Refresher

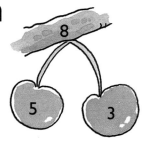

1 Partition the 6, 7, 8, or 9 into "5 and a bit" and then complete the calculations.

**Example**
a 15 + 8
  15 + 5 + 3

b 15 + 7     c 15 + 9

d 25 + 6    e 25 + 8

f 25 + 7    g 35 + 9

h 35 + 6    i 35 + 8

## Practice

1 Partition both numbers into "5 and a bit" and then complete the calculations.

**Example**
a 27 + 9
  25 + 2 + 5 + 4

b 28 + 7    c 26 + 8

d 39 + 6    e 46 + 9

f 47 + 8    g 58 + 9

h 48 + 7    i 57 + 6    j 66 + 8

k 68 + 8    l 79 + 7    m 16 + 27

n 26 + 18    o 19 + 36

Frank's fresh fruit

12

# Balloon hundreds

## Refresher

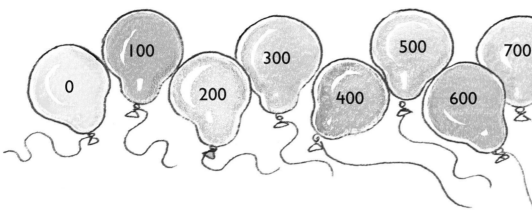

1   Write out the multiples of 100 to 1000
    100, 200, ... 1000

2   Write the next multiple of 100.

    **a** 600, 700       **b** 300           **c** 500           **d** 100
    **e** 900          **f** 0             **g** 200           **h** 700

3   Write the previous multiple of 100.

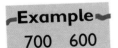

| Example | |
|---|---|
| 700 | 600 |

    **b** 900        **c** 400        **d** 200
    **e** 1000      **f** 300       **g** 800
    **h** 600

## Practice

**Example**
600 + 400
6 + 4

1   Write out the calculation, filling in the missing 100.
    Now look at the calculations again and write the
    number fact for 10 that helps you remember it.

    **a** _____ + 800 = 1000        **b** 400 + _____ = 1000

    **c** 900 + _____ = 1000        **d** 500 + _____ = 1000

    **e** 700 + _____ = 1000        **f** _____ + 1000 = 1000

    **g** _____ + 400 = 1000        **h** 100 + _____ = 1000

    **i** 200 + _____ = 1000        **j** _____ + 300 = 1000

# Football fives

## Refresher

1   Write out all the multiples of 5 to 100.
5, 10, 15…100

2   Write the next multiple of 5.
a  50, 55      b  80          c  30          d  60          e  10

3   Write the previous multiple of 5.
a  30          b  70          c  40          d  100         e  50

4   Copy out the calculations, filling in the missing multiple of 10.

a   20 + ☐ = 100        b   50 + ☐ = 100        c   ☐ + 70 = 100

d   90 + ☐ = 100        e   40 + ☐ = 100        f   ☐ + 20 = 100

## Practice

1   Write out the calculations, filling in the missing multiple of 5.
Now go through the calculations again and write the pair
of multiples of 10 that help you remember it.

**Example**
65 + 35 = 100
60 + 40 = 100

a   95 + ☐ = 100        b   45 + ☐ = 100        c   ☐ + 75 = 100

d   85 + ☐ = 100        e   65 + ☐ = 100        f   5 + ☐ = 100

g   ☐ + 25 = 100        h   ☐ + 15 = 100        i   ☐ + 55 = 100

# Jump to 1000

**A game for 2 players**

100

200

300

400

500

600

700

800

900

1000 Collect a counter!

## How to play:

● Place your counters on 100.
● Take turns to throw the die. Each number means that many hundreds. If you throw 4, it means 400.
● The aim of the game is to try to jump to 1000.
● You can move in any direction. If you land on 1000, collect a counter.
● The first player to collect 5 counters is the winner.

### Refresher

You will need: a 1–10 die     a counter for each player

a list of the pairs of multiples of 100         10 counters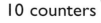

### Practice

You will need: a 1–10 die     a counter for each player

10 counters

# Cake tray problems

## Refresher

Mr Baker has made 12 currant buns and 8 jam tarts.

1 How many cakes does Mr Baker have to sell altogether?

2 Sam buys 5 jam tarts. How many are left?

3 Emma buys six currant buns for her and her sister to share. How many do they have each?

4 Tomorrow Mr Baker will bake double the number of buns and tarts . How many will he bake altogether?

Remember: Show all your workings out

## Practice

William, Tim and Amy bought sweets for three weeks. William has 18, Tim has 8 more and Amy has twice as many as William.

1 How many sweets do William and Tim have altogether?

2 Every week William bought the same number of sweets. How many did he buy each week?

3 Amy shares her sweets with William and Tim. How many do they each get?

4 How many more sweets do William and Tim need together to have the same number as Amy?

# Delicious problems

## Refresher

Tom has £1 to spend at the mini-market.

1  How much would he pay for crisps and a chocolate bar?

2  How much would he pay for a drink and bubble gum?

3  Tom buys a bag of crisps and pays with a 50p coin. How much change does he get?

4  Tom buys a drink and pays with a £1 coin. How much change does he get?

## Practice

Jim has £3·50 to spend at the newsagent and Rose has £4·50.

1  How much more does Rose have than Jim?

2  Rose spends half of her money on a game. How much does she spend?

3  Jim buys some pencils and a packet of stickers. He pays with a £2 coin. How much change does he get?

4  Rose buys 2 packets of pens and pays with 3 coins. Which coins did she use?

# Building tetrominoid city

## Refresher

1 Use four cubes each time to build these tetrominoid houses.

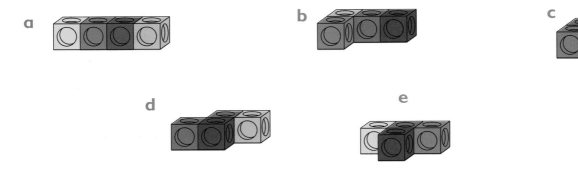

a b c

d e

## Practice

1 Use cubes to build these houses for tetrominoids.

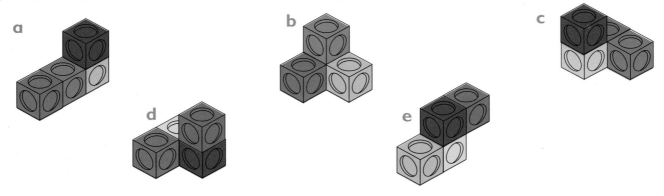

a b c

d e

2 Some tetrominoids decided to add a one cube extension to their designs.
Use your cubes to build these houses.

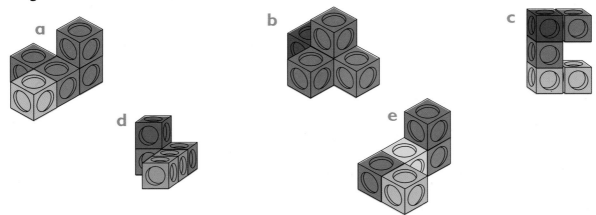

a b c

d e

3 Now build your own houses. Using five cubes, build five new shapes.

# Shaping up

You will need:
regular 2D shapes with congruent sides

**~Example~**

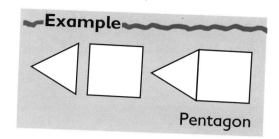

Pentagon

## Refresher

1  Find which pairs of 2D shapes make these shapes. Name each shape.

a 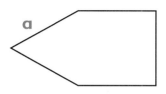   b 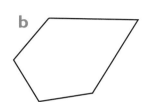   c    d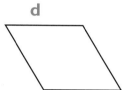

## Practice

1  Take two triangles and one regular shape.
Fit the three shapes together to match
these outlines. Name each new shape.

a  **~Example~**

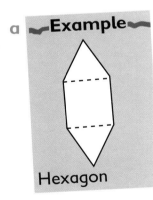

Hexagon

b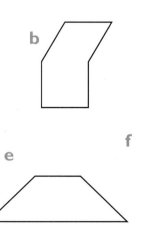

c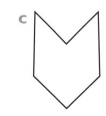

d

e

f    g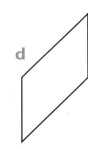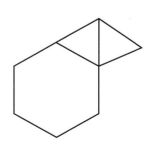

2  Fit together the following shapes.

a  4 △ and 1 □ to make a four-pointed star.

b  5 △ and 1 ⬠ to make a five-pointed star.

c  6 △ and 1 ⬡ to make a six-pointed star.

19

# Rocket patterns

You will need:

3 rectangles – I red, I blue and I yellow

## Refresher

I  Fit your rectangles in to the rocket outline to make different patterns.

Here is one way.      Can you find five more?

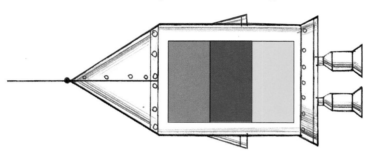

## Practice

I  Fit your rectangles into the rocket outline, using one of the following patterns.

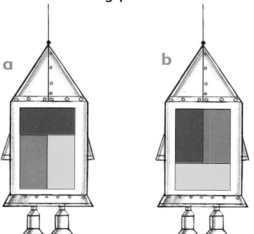

a      b

How many different ways can you fit your three rectangles in to the rocket outline? Think of a way to record your answers. Here is an example.

blue

red  yellow

# Template patterns

## Refresher

1 Make one of these templates.
   a Tape two identical shapes along touching sides like this, or along partially touching sides like this.
   b Draw round the outline of your template. Now draw more outlines and try to make them fit together.
   c Use coloured pencils to decorate your pattern.

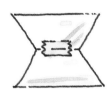 
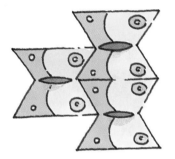 

## Practice

1 Make a template like this.
   a Draw round a plastic square. Cut out the square shape.
   b Cut a semi-circle from one side. Slide it to the opposite side and tape it in place.
   c Now cut out a triangle from one of the other sides. Slide it across the shape and tape it in place.
   d Draw round the outline of your template several times to make a pattern with the outlines fitting together. Use coloured pencils to decorate your pattern.

  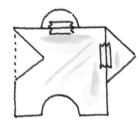

# Helicopter directions

## Refresher

You are in a helicopter hovering over Alpha rig. Look at the map then copy and complete these sentences.

1 I can see _____ rig to the south.

2 I can see _____ rig to the east.

3 The supply ship is to the _____

4 If I want to fly to the Aberton Port, I will have to face _____

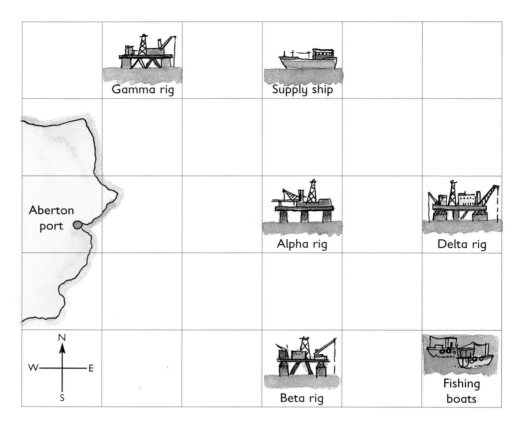

## Practice

Write the answers to these questions.

1 I am hovering over an oil rig. I can see the supply ship in front of me. Behind me is Beta rig.
   a In which direction am I facing?
   b If I make a quarter turn to the right, which oil rig will I see?

2 I am flying over the fishing boats. Behind me is Beta rig.
   a In which direction am I flying?
   b I want to land on Delta rig. Write down the directions.

3 In front of me is Gamma rig and to the south is Alpha rig.
   a Where am I?
   b In which direction am I flying?

4 I am hovering over an oil rig. I can see Aberton Port in front of me. Behind me is Delta rig.
   a In which direction am I facing?
   b If I make a quarter turn to the left, which rig will I see?

# Wild West directions

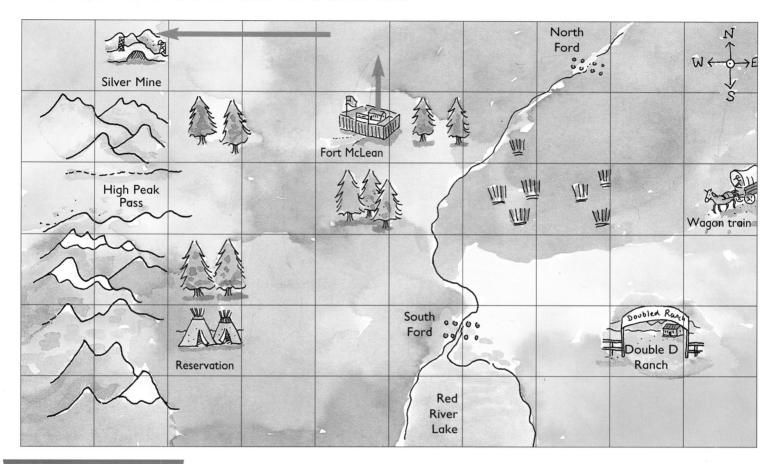

## Refresher

1 You are at Fort McLean. Where do these directions take you?
   a 1 square north, 3 squares west.
   b 1 square west, 1 square south, 2 squares west.
   c 1 square west, 3 squares south, 1 square west.
   d 1 square north, 4 squares east, 4 squares south.

**Key:**

| dangerous | safe |
| --- | --- |
| swamp | ford |
| forest | |

## Practice

1 You are with the wagon train. There are some dangers on the trail which you must avoid. You can only cross the Red River at a ford.
   a Find a safe route to Fort McLean.
   b The wagon train is headed for the High Peaks Pass in the mountains. Work out a safe route.
   c Write a route from the Double D Ranch to the silver mine.

# Robot 1, 2, 3

## Refresher

1 A robot began this pattern... then ran out of ink!

a Copy this 1, 2, 3 pattern on to squared paper.
Start near the middle of the paper.

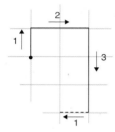

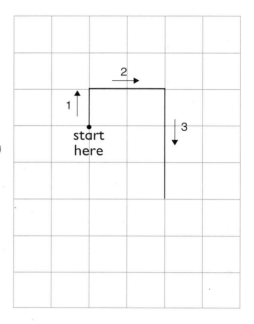

b Repeat the pattern
four times starting where the
last pattern ends each time.

## Practice

1 You will need a sheet of squared paper.
Fold the sheet in half and mark a starting
dot on each half sheet.

a Copy the robot pattern 1, 4, 2.
Repeat it four times.

b Copy the robot pattern 2, 4, 1.
Repeat it four times.

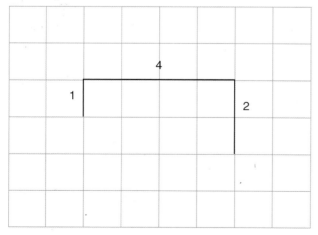

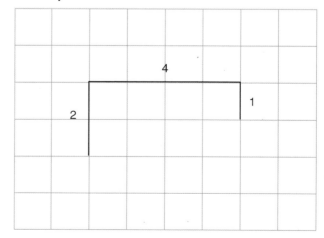

2 Look at your completed patterns.

a Write how the two patterns are the same. b Write how the two patterns are different.

3 Make up a pattern of your own.

24

# Time out

## Refresher

1 Copy and complete these five minute patterns.
  a 3:00, 3:05, 3:10, _____, _____, _____, 3:30.
  b 4:25, 4:30, 4:35, _____, _____, _____, _____.
  c 8:45, 8:50, _____, _____, _____, _____.

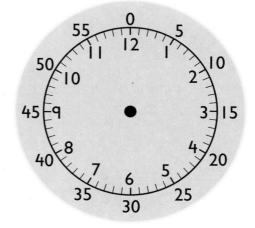

2 Write the time these clocks show in digital form.

a

b

c

## Practice

1 Write these times in two ways.

  a **7:40**  b **9:55**  c **1:35**  d **6:50**  e **12:45**

**Example**

7:40
40 minutes past 7
20 minutes to 8

2 These children have check-up appointments with the school dentist.

Mark's appointment is at **3:45**
Write the appointment time for
  a Emma, 10 minutes before Mark
  b Neil, 10 minutes after Mark
  c Omar, 20 minutes before Mark
  d Rachel, 20 minutes after Mark.

3 Write these appointment times in order, starting with the earliest.
  10:00 a.m.   9:05 a.m.   4:25 p.m.   11:40 a.m.   1:50 p.m.   12:35 p.m.

25

# Weigh it up

## Refresher

1 Write the weight of each item to the nearest kilogram.

a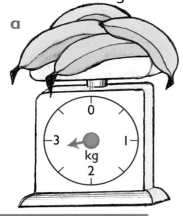

c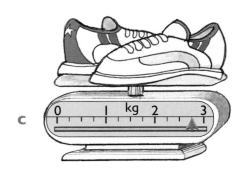

d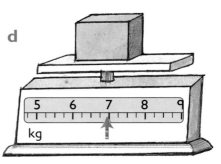

## Practice

1 Write the weight of each parcel to the nearest half kilogram.

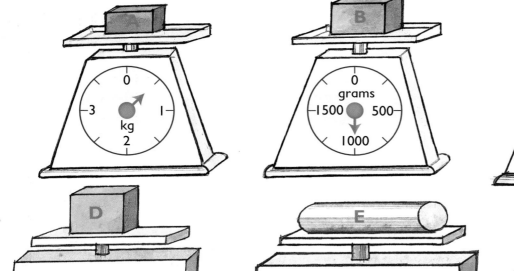

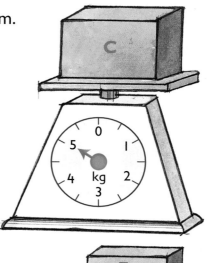

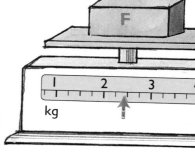

2 Write the letter of the parcel which is

a $\frac{1}{2}$ kg heavier than parcel A

b 4 kg heavier than parcel B

c $3\frac{1}{2}$ kg lighter than parcel C

d 1 kg heavier than parcel D

e the same weight as parcel E

f double the weight of parcel F

# Easter egg weights

## Refresher

1 These children each found $\frac{1}{2}$ kg of eggs in the Easter Egg Hunt.
Copy and complete the table to show the weights of the eggs that each child found.

| Child | 200g | 100g |
|-------|------|------|
| Keri | 2 | 1 |
| Kevin | | 3 |
| Kitty | | |

I found two 200 g eggs and one 100 g egg. That's 500 g altogether.

## Practice

1 These children each found 1 kg of eggs in the Easter Egg Hunt. Copy and complete the table.

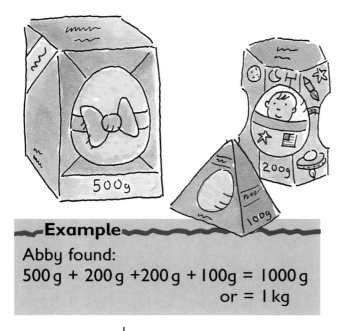

**Example**

Abby found:
500 g + 200 g + 200 g + 100 g = 1000 g
                           or = 1 kg

2 Rob found $1\frac{1}{2}$ kg of eggs.
The heaviest egg weighed 500 g.
Find three different combinations of eggs whose total weight is $1\frac{1}{2}$ kg.

| Child | 500g | 200g | 100g |
|-------|------|------|------|
| Abby | 1 | 2 | 1 |
| Bert | 1 | | 3 |
| Cindy | 0 | 4 | |
| Dan | 0 | | 6 |
| Eli | | 0 | 0 |
| Fran | 0 | | 0 |
| Jill | 1 | 0 | |
| Hetty | 0 | | 4 |
| Iyaz | 0 | 1 | |
| Jenny | 0 | 0 | |

# Ready steady cookery

## Refresher

1  Look at the recipe for 4 people.
   a  Write a scrambled eggs recipe for 2 people.
   b  Now write the recipe for 8 people.

**Scrambled eggs recipe**

6 large eggs
200 g bacon
100 g mushrooms
50 g butter
salt and pepper

I need to double the quantities.

## Practice

1  These recipes are for 4 people.

2 people will need half as much as 4.

**Seafood pasta**

400 g pasta
300 g mussels
200 g prawns
500 g plum tomatoes
20 g chilli pepper
100 g parmesan cheese
2 cloves garlic

**Singapore rice noodles**

200 g rice noodles
125 g cooked chicken
50 g prawns
100 g beansprouts
30 g onion
60 g oil

I opened a 500 g pack of rice noodles to cook the meal for eight people. What is the weight of the noodles left?

a  Write the seafood pasta recipe for 2 people.
b  Write the Singapore rice noodles recipe for 8 people.

# Puppy weights

**Glenbrae Vets: clinic records**

Parents: Dot and Dash

Puppies: Daisy, Dixie, Dolly

Puppy weights: 2 months

|       | kg | g   |
|-------|----|-----|
| Daisy | 5  | 500 |
| Dixie | 6  | 500 |
| Dolly | 4  | 500 |

Puppy weights: 4 months

|       | kg | g   |
|-------|----|-----|
| Daisy | 12 | 500 |
| Dixie | 12 | 0   |
| Dolly | 11 | 500 |

Puppy weights: 6 months

|       | kg | g   |
|-------|----|-----|
| Daisy | 16 | 800 |
| Dixie | 17 | 600 |
| Dolly | 16 | 500 |

## Refresher

1  Copy and complete the weight for each puppy at 2 months.
   Daisy weighs _____kg and _____g, or _____kg.
   Dixie weighs _____kg and _____g, or _____kg.
   Dolly weighs _____kg and _____g, or _____kg.

2  Copy and complete the weight for each puppy at 4 months.
   Daisy weighs _____kg and _____g, or _____kg.
   Dixie weighs _____kg and _____g, or _____kg.
   Dolly weighs _____kg and _____g, or _____kg.

## Practice

1  At 6 months, which puppy is
   a the heaviest?
   b 300 g lighter than Daisy?
   c 200 g less than 17 kg?

2  Look at the weights for 2 months and 6 months.
   Work out how much weight each puppy has gained.

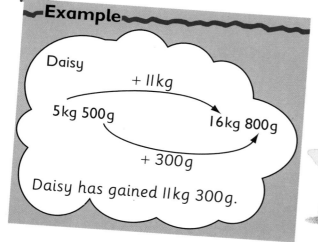

**Example**

Daisy

+ 11kg

5kg 500g → 16kg 800g

+ 300g

Daisy has gained 11kg 300g.

DAISY    DIXIE    DOLLY

29

# Weighty problems

## Refresher

1 Write the better estimate of weight for each of these.

a a new-born baby

3 kg or 30 kg

b a mouse

30 g or 300 g

c

5 kg or 50 kg

d a dalmatian dog

25 kg or 250 kg

e a cow

70 kg or 700 kg

f an elephant

60 kg or 6000 kg

## Practice

**Example**

1 egg ⟶ 50 g
2 eggs ⟶ 100 g
4 eggs ⟶ 200 g } 6 eggs ⟶ ? g

1 Solve these problems. Write down how you worked out the answers.

a An egg weighs about 50 g.
About how much do 6 eggs weigh?

b The weight of a large loaf is 800 g.
How much will 3 loaves weigh?

c A box of 6 cheese triangles
weighs 180 g. Tom uses 3 triangles
of cheese for his sandwiches. What
weight of cheese is left in the box?

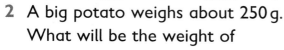

d A pack of 4 scones weighs 240 g.
What does 1 scone weigh?

2 A big potato weighs about 250 g.
What will be the weight of

a 4 big potatoes?

b 8 big potatoes?

c 10 big potatoes?

# Jack and the beanstalk 3s

## Refresher

1 Copy and complete the number sequence to show the multiples of 3.

 3  6   12   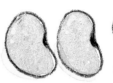   30

2 Write the multiple of 3 that comes after these numbers.

   a  12        d  24
   b  18        e  9
   c  6         f  30

3 Write the multiple of 3 that comes before these numbers.

   a  6         d  27
   b  30        e  9
   c  15        f  33

## Practice

1 Copy and complete the number sequences by adding or subtracting 3 for each step Jack takes.

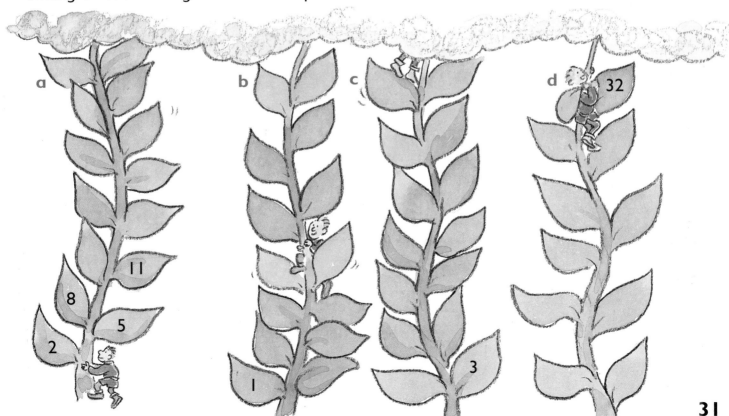

a 11 8 5 2    b 1    c 3    d 32

31

# Bus ride 4s

## Refresher

1 Copy and complete the number sequence to show the multiples of 4.

| 4 | 8 | | | 20 | | | | | 40 |

2 Write the multiple of 4 that comes after these numbers.

a  8        d  40

b  16       e  32

c  24       f  4

3 Write the multiple of 4 that comes before these numbers.

a  20       d  36

b  8        e  40

c  16       f  24

## Practice

1 Count in 4s to find out how many people are on the bus after each stop. Write each number.

a  3 people

b  10 people

c  17 people

d  24 people

7    11

32

# Counting blocks

## Refresher

1  Add or subtract the number shown on the
   blocks to complete the number sequences.

   a  +4  2, 6, ——, ——, 18, ——, ——, 30

   b  +5  3, 8, 13, ——, ——, ——, ——, ——

   c  +3  1, 4, ——, ——, ——, ——, 19, ——

   d  −5  50, 45, 40, ——, ——, ——, ——, ——

   e  −4  40, 36, ——, ——, ——, ——, ——, ——,

## Practice

1
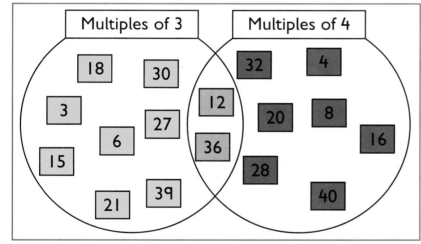

The number cards have been
sorted into multiples of 3 and
multiples of 4.
Three cards are missing. What
are the missing numbers and
where do they belong?

2  Draw your own sorting circles like the ones below.
   Sort the numbers 1–40 to match the labels. Write
   any numbers that belong in both sets in the middle.

   a 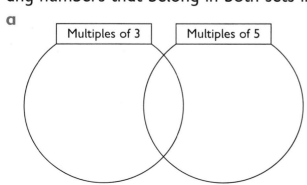   b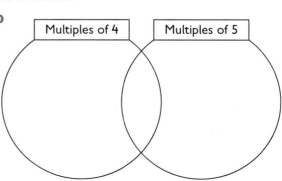

# Patterns of 3

## Refresher

If we add the digits together they always end up being a 3, 6 or 9.
24 ➝ 2 + 4 = 6
39 ➝ 3 + 9 = 12

0 1 2 3 4 5 6 7 8 9 10 11 12 13 14 15 16 17 18 19 20 21 22 23 24 25 26 27 28 29 30 31 32 33 34 35 36 37 38 39 40 41 42 43 44 45 46 47 48 49 50

1  Using a number line, draw jumps of 3, starting from 1.
2  Using a number line, draw jumps of 3, starting from 2.

# Investigation

## Practice

Try this investigation.

1  Starting from 1, count in 3s up to about 60. Write the numbers under each other. Add the digits in each of the numbers. Continue adding the digits until you have a single-digit number. What do you notice?

2  Starting from 2 and counting in 3s up to about 60, write the numbers as before. What do you notice?

# Investigating 3s and 5s

## Refresher

The children in Year 3 carried out an investigation. They added 3s and 5s to make all of the numbers between 10 and 20. Here are their results.

Continue the investigation to see if you can make the numbers between 21 and 30.

**Year 3 Investigation**

| 10 | → | 5 + 5 |
|----|---|-------|
| 11 | → | 3 + 3 + 5 |
| 12 | → | 3 + 3 + 3 + 3 |
| 13 | → | 3 + 5 + 5 |
| 14 | → | 3 + 3 + 3 + 5 |
| 15 | → | 5 + 5 + 5 |
| 16 | → | 5 + 5 + 3 + 3 |
| 17 | → | 3 + 3 + 3 + 3 + 5 |
| 18 | → | 3 + 5 + 5 + 5 |
| 19 | → | 5 + 5 + 3 + 3 + 3 |
| 20 | → | 5 + 5 + 5 + 5 |

## Practice

Carry out your own investigations like the one above.

### Investigation

What numbers can you make by adding 3s and 4s together?

Can you make all of the numbers between 7 and 30?

1  What is the smallest total you can make using the numbers 3 and 4? Is it possible to make the numbers up to 30?

### Investigation

What numbers can you make by adding 2s and 5s together?

Can you make all of the numbers between 7 and 30?

2  What is the smallest total you can make using the numbers 2 and 5? Is it possible to make the numbers up to 30?

# Fast facts

## Refresher

1 Partition the numbers, then add them together.

a 23 + 15 = ☐     b 13 + 24 = ☐

c 11 + 25 = ☐     d 27 + 22 = ☐

e 26 + 32 = ☐     f 34 + 35 = ☐

g 41 + 37 = ☐     h 46 + 23 = ☐

This is how I worked it out. Remember: show all your workings-out.

31 + 16 =

30 + 1 + 10 + 6

30 + 10 + 6 + 1 = 47

## Practice

1 Add the numbers mentally. Show how you worked them out.

36 + 52 = 50 + 30 + 6 + 2

36 + 52 = 88

50 + 30 + 6 + 2

a 47 + 75 = ☐

b 29 + 34 = ☐

c 55 + 42 = ☐

d 67 + 31 = ☐

e 55 + 68 = ☐

f 97 + 85 = ☐

g 81 + 69 = ☐

h 78 + 64 = ☐

● Extend understanding that more than two numbers can be added; add three or four two-digit numbers with the help of apparatus or pencil and paper

Sp 8, 2

# Bead calculations

## Refresher

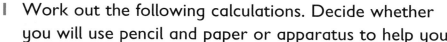

1 Work out the following calculations. Decide whether you will use pencil and paper or apparatus to help you.

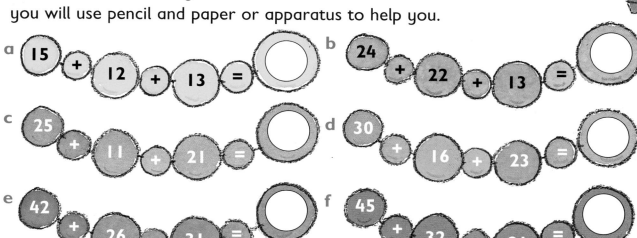

a  15 + 12 + 13 = ◯

b  24 + 22 + 13 = ◯

c  25 + 11 + 21 = ◯

d  30 + 16 + 23 = ◯

e  42 + 26 + 31 = ◯

f  45 + 32 + 21 = ◯

g  24 + 52 + 33 = ◯

h  62 + 25 + 32 = ◯

## Practice

1 Work out the following calculations. Decide whether you will use pencil and paper or apparatus to help you.

Remember: Show all your workings-out.

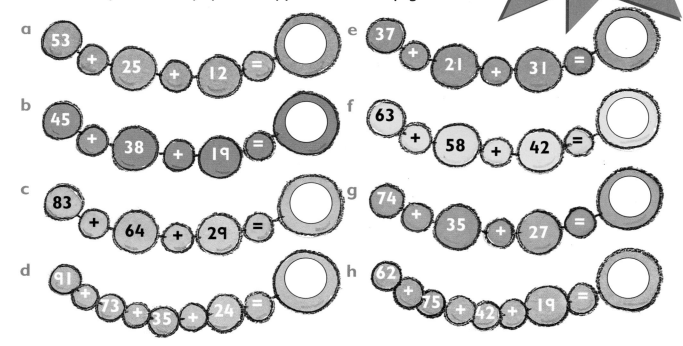

a  53 + 25 + 12 = ◯

e  37 + 21 + 31 = ◯

b  45 + 38 + 19 = ◯

f  63 + 58 + 42 = ◯

c  83 + 64 + 29 = ◯

g  74 + 35 + 27 = ◯

d  91 + 73 + 35 + 24 = ◯

h  62 + 75 + 42 + 19 = ◯

37

# Animal addition

## Refresher

1 Use the numbers on the animals and add three of them together. Use paper and pencil or apparatus to help you. How many different totals can you find?

*You should find four totals for each set of numbers.*

a 12 15 31 42

b 34 14 43 21

c 52 11 35 23

## Practice

1 Use the numbers on the animals and add four of them together. How many different totals can you find?

*You should find five totals for each set of numbers.*

a 36 22 57 45 61

b 82 17 29 38 53

c 52 87 34 27 98

# Fish and bone problems

## Refresher

Today, Max the cat has 15 fish and 8 sausages.

1   How many things does Max have altogether?
2   Max gives five fish to his friend Mitch. How many fish does he have left?
3   Max shares the fish he has left with his friend Prince. How many do they have each?
4   Tomorrow, Max wants to get double the number of sausages. How many will he have?

## Practice

Patch the dog has 24 bones. His friend Topper has half as many.

1   Patch has found 3 bones every week. How many weeks has he been finding them?
2   How many bones do Patch and Topper have altogether?
3   If Patch shares his bones between him and five friends, how many do they each get?
4   Patch and Topper want to collect 100 bones each. How many more do they need altogether?

# Divide by...?

## Refresher

1 Write a division fact for each of these pictures.

a

$$20 \div 2 = 10$$

c

d

e

f

## Practice

1 Write two multiplication and two division facts for each of these pictures.

a

**Example**

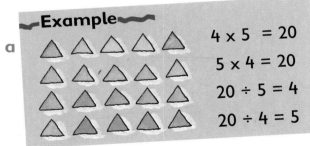

$$4 \times 5 = 20$$
$$5 \times 4 = 20$$
$$20 \div 5 = 4$$
$$20 \div 4 = 5$$

b

c

d

e

e

40

# Fruit bowl division

## Refresher

**Example**

6 × 2 = 12

1  Multiply the numbers on each piece
of fruit by the number on the bowl.

a    b    c

## Practice

1  Write two multiplication and two division facts for each fruit.

a  **Example**

4 × 2 = 8
2 × 4 = 8
8 ÷ 2 = 4
8 ÷ 4 = 2

b    c

d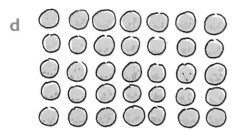

e     f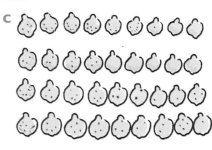

2  Write two multiplication and two division facts for each set of cards.

a

| 6 | 2 | 12 |

b

| 8 | 10 | 80 |

c

| 7 | 5 | 35 |

d

| 9 | 5 | 45 |

# Flower stall division

## Refresher

1 Match the multiplication fact with its division fact.

| $3 \times 4 = 12$ | $8 \times 10 = 80$ | $6 \times 5 = 30$ | $7 \times 2 = 14$ | $5 \times 3 = 15$ | $10 \times 4 = 40$ |

| $80 \div 10 = 8$ | $14 \div 2 = 7$ | $40 \div 4 = 10$ | $15 \div 3 = 5$ | $12 \div 4 = 3$ | $30 \div 5 = 6$ |

## Practice

1 Write a division number sentence for each of these problems.
  Check to see you have answered the question.

a Ricky buys 25 roses. He gives the same number of roses to his five friends. How many roses do they each get?

b Fran spends £12. She buys 3 lilies. How much does each lily cost?

c The headteacher buys 80 sunflowers. She gives 10 to each class. How many classes are there?

d Ruksana buys 21 tulips. She puts 7 in each vase. How many vases does she need?

e Buttercups come in bunches of 5. Mr Ahmed buys a total of 35 buttercups. How many bunches did he buy?

f Daisies cost £20 for 10. How much does 1 daisy cost?

● Solve word problems involving numbers in "real life"

Sp 9, 3

# What's the problem?

1 Write the answer to these division facts.

a
20 ÷ 5 = ☐
30 ÷ 10 = ☐
12 ÷ 2 = ☐
35 ÷ 5 = ☐

b
16 ÷ 4 = ☐
9 ÷ 3 = ☐
4 ÷ 2 = ☐
25 ÷ 5 = ☐

c
100 ÷ 10 = ☐
40 ÷ 5 = ☐
18 ÷ 2 = ☐
12 ÷ 3 = ☐

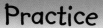

Practice

1 Work out the answers to these problems in your head then write down the answer.

a A chocolate bar costs 5p. How many can you buy for 45p?

b Put 24 cakes into 4 bags. How many cakes in each bag?

c 3 biscuits cost 27p altogether. How much did each cost?

d 8 children ate 16 doughnuts. How many doughnuts each?

2 Make jottings as you work through these problems. Use the answers to make your final calculation.

a Sam gets £5 pocket money per week. He wants to buy a football for £20 and a computer game for £25. How many weeks will it take him to save enough money?

b James and Mary collect stamps. James has 15 and Mary has 13. They put 7 stamps on each page of their album. How many pages do they use?

3 Write all of the calculations necessary to answer these problems.

a Roses cost £15 for 5. Daffodils cost £8 for 4. Sunflowers cost £20 for 4. Mrs Singh buys 1 of each flower. How much does she spend?

b How much more does it cost to buy 8 books for £5 each than 9 calculators for £3 each?

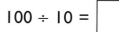

43

● Derive quickly doubles of all whole numbers to at least 20 and multiples of 5 to 100 and 50 to 500 and the corresponding halves

Sp 9, 4

# Rainy day doubles and halves

## Refresher

1 Double each number.

50   300
5
17
20   80
150

2 Halve each number.

50
20   24
100
80   400
16

## Practice

1 Halve each number that falls on to the umbrella to get the new number.

**Example**

28  Halve me  14

a

22   28
64   50
34

Halve me

b

90   140   170
80
110

Halve me

c

1000   600
700
900   500

Halve me

d

85   45
65   35

Double me

e

13   18
16   11

Double me

f

250
450
350   150

Double me

44

# Starry doubles

## Refresher

**Example**
7 + 7 = 14
14 + 14 = 28

1  Double the number on each star and then double it again.

16    15    30    12

7    10    8    18    25    9

## Practice

1  Complete each number fact for 2 on the outside of each card.
   Open the card to find a number fact for 4. Double your first
   answer to complete the fact for 4.

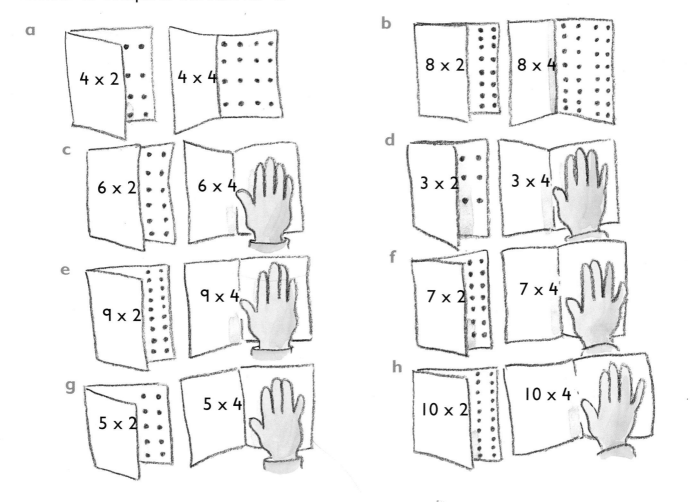

a    4 x 2    4 x 4

b    8 x 2    8 x 4

c    6 x 2    6 x 4

d    3 x 2    3 x 4

e    9 x 2    9 x 4

f    7 x 2    7 x 4

g    5 x 2    5 x 4

h    10 x 2    10 x 4

# Wall and window fractions

1 What fraction of the windows have been frosted over?

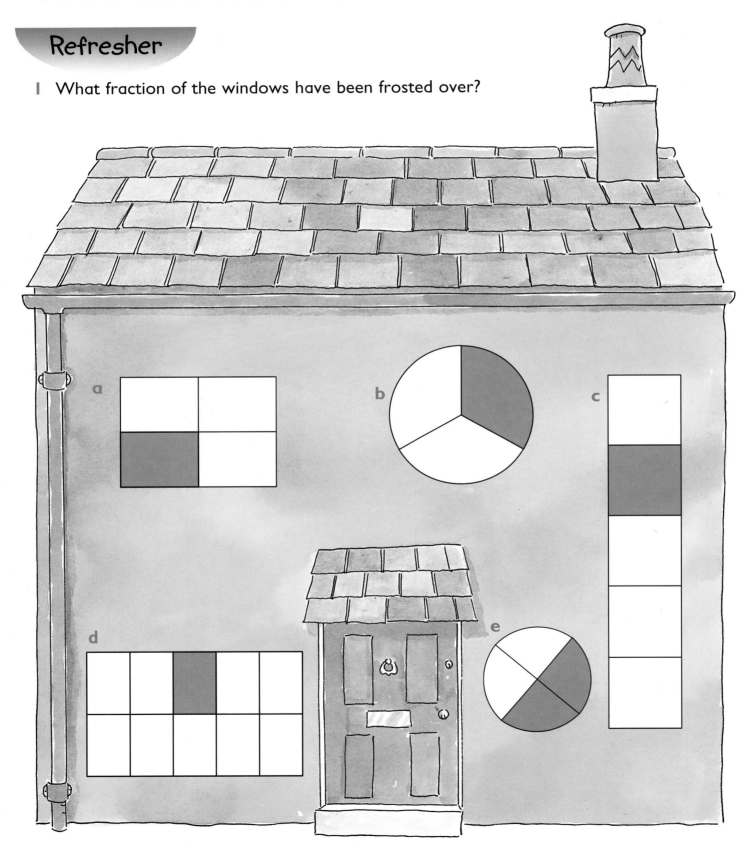

## Practice

1  What fraction of the wall has fallen down?

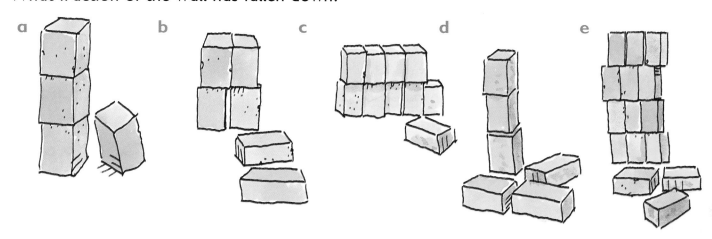

a    b    c    d    e

2  A fraction of each wall has been built. Build the wall using the correct number of bricks.
   Write the number of bricks needed to build the whole wall.

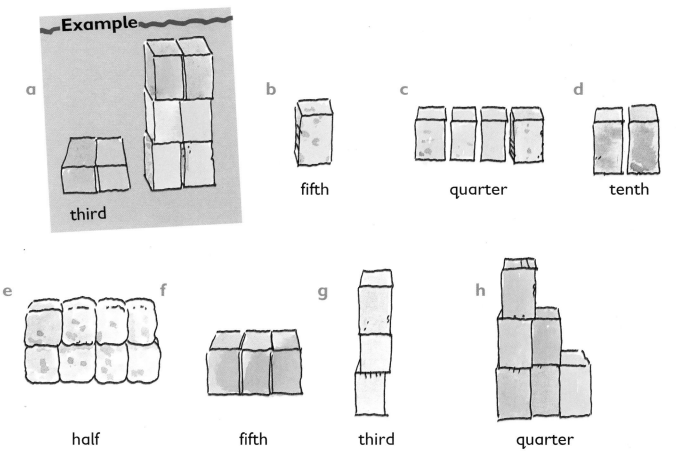

**Example**

a    third

b    fifth

c    quarter

d    tenth

e    half

f    fifth

g    third

h    quarter

# Teatime halves and quarters

## Refresher

1 Copy each cake. Colour half red, a quarter blue and a quarter yellow. Write $\frac{1}{2}$ or $\frac{1}{4}$ on the correct sections.

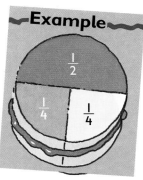
Example

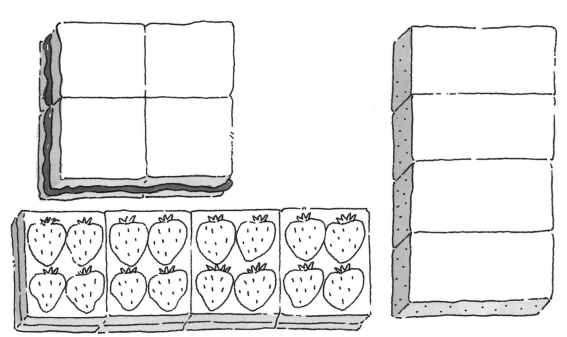

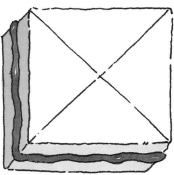

2 Ben gets half the biscuits. Amir and Emma get a quarter each. How many does each child get?

48

## Practice

1 Join the halves and quarters to make whole cakes.
Write down the letters that make a whole cake.
Then write the fractions that make each whole cake.

2 Gurjit gets half the biscuits. Zoe and Ann get a
quarter each. How many does each child get?
Use counters to help you.

# Plasticine fractions

## Refresher

| Write down the fraction for each plasticine shape.

a
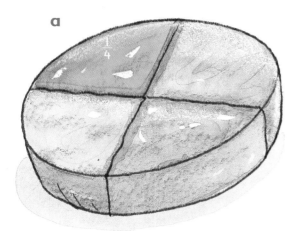

b

c
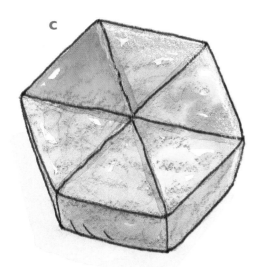

d
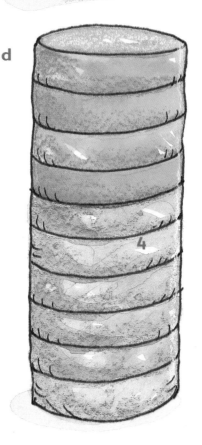

## Practice

1 Write down the fraction that has been squashed.

a $\frac{1}{2}$

b $\frac{4}{5}$

c $\frac{2}{3}$

d $\frac{1}{4}$

e $\frac{2}{5}$

f $\frac{2}{5}$    $\frac{2}{5}$

g $\frac{1}{4}$    $\frac{1}{4}$

h $\frac{2}{5}$    $\frac{1}{5}$

i $\frac{2}{10}$    $\frac{4}{10}$

j $\frac{3}{10}$    $\frac{2}{10}$    $\frac{3}{10}$

**51**

# Freezing fractions

## Refresher

1  What fraction of the tray has ice cubes?
2  What fraction of the tray is empty?

a

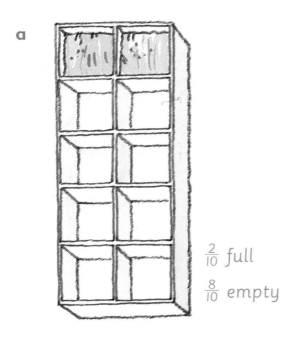

$\frac{2}{10}$ full

$\frac{8}{10}$ empty

b

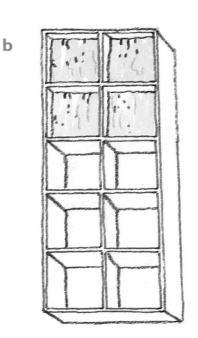

c

d

e

## Practice

1 Which trays are half filled with ice cubes?

a        b        c        d        e

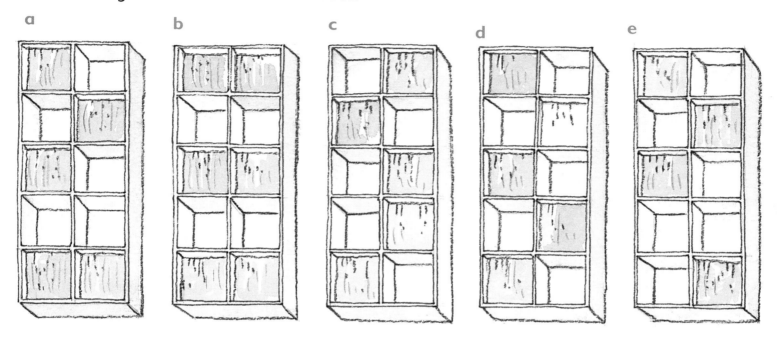

2 Sharna wants each lolly to be half red. What
fraction of juice must she add or pour out?

a        b        c        d        e        f

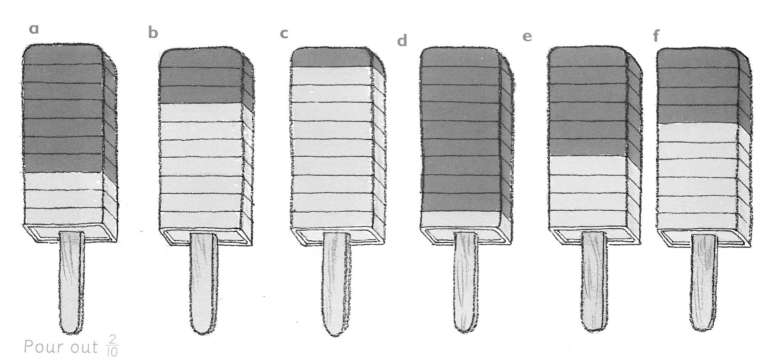

Pour out $\frac{2}{10}$

**53**

# Plate fractions

## Refresher

1   Write down two fractions for each plate.

a

b

c

d

e

## Practice

**1** Write down the fraction that is needed to make a whole plate.

a $\frac{1}{4}$

b $\frac{3}{10}$

c $\frac{1}{2}$

d $\frac{3}{5}$

e $\frac{2}{10}$

f $\frac{5}{10}$

g $\frac{2}{5}$

h $\frac{3}{4}$

i $\frac{7}{10}$

**2 a** Write down two fractions that make half.
  **b** Write down three fractions that make a whole.
  **c** Write down four fractions that make a whole.

**55**

● Solve a given problem by organising and interpreting numerical data in simple lists, tables and graphs, for example, bar charts

Sp 11, 1

# Window bar chart

## Refresher

1  Count the windows for each colour.
Copy and complete the table.

| Colour | Number |
| --- | --- |
| Red | |
| Blue | |
| Yellow | |
| Black | |
| Orange | |

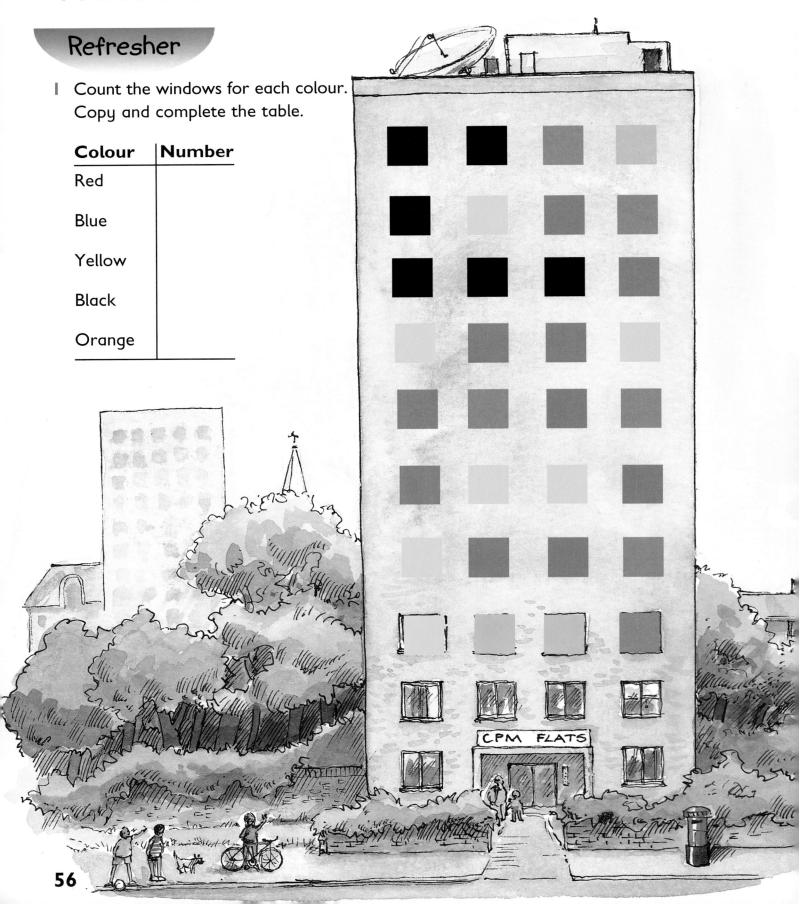

CPM FLATS

## Practice

1  Copy and complete bar chart for the table on page 56.

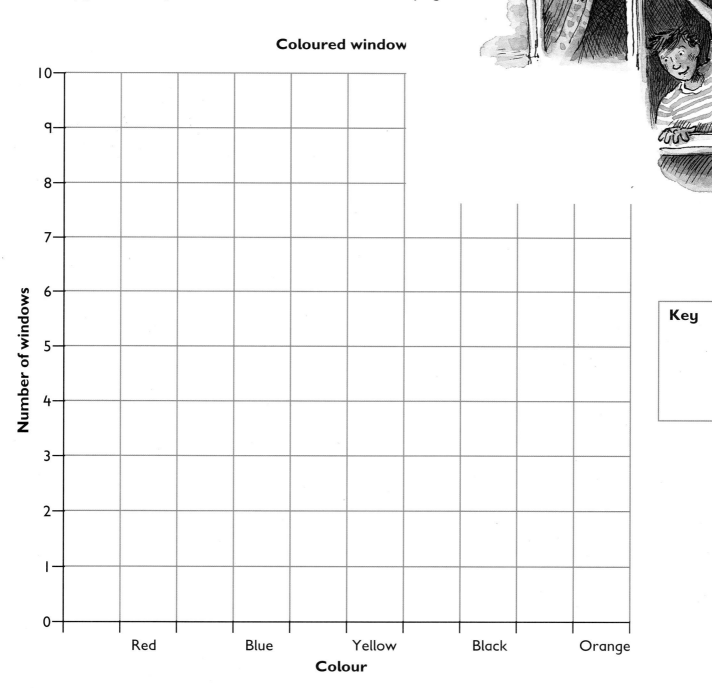

**Coloured window**

Key

*Number of windows* (y-axis: 0, 1, 2, 3, 4, 5, 6, 7, 8, 9, 10)

*Colour* (x-axis: Red, Blue, Yellow, Black, Orange)

1  Which colour is most common?
2  There are more blue than red windows. How many more?
3  How many windows are not blue?

● Solve a given problem by organising and interpreting numerical data in simple lists, tables and graphs, for example, bar charts

Sp 11, 2

# Flower charts

## Refresher

1 Count the flowers of each colour. Copy and complete the table. Now copy and complete the bar chart.

| Colour | Number |
|--------|--------|
| Red    |        |
| Yellow |        |
| Blue   |        |
| Orange |        |

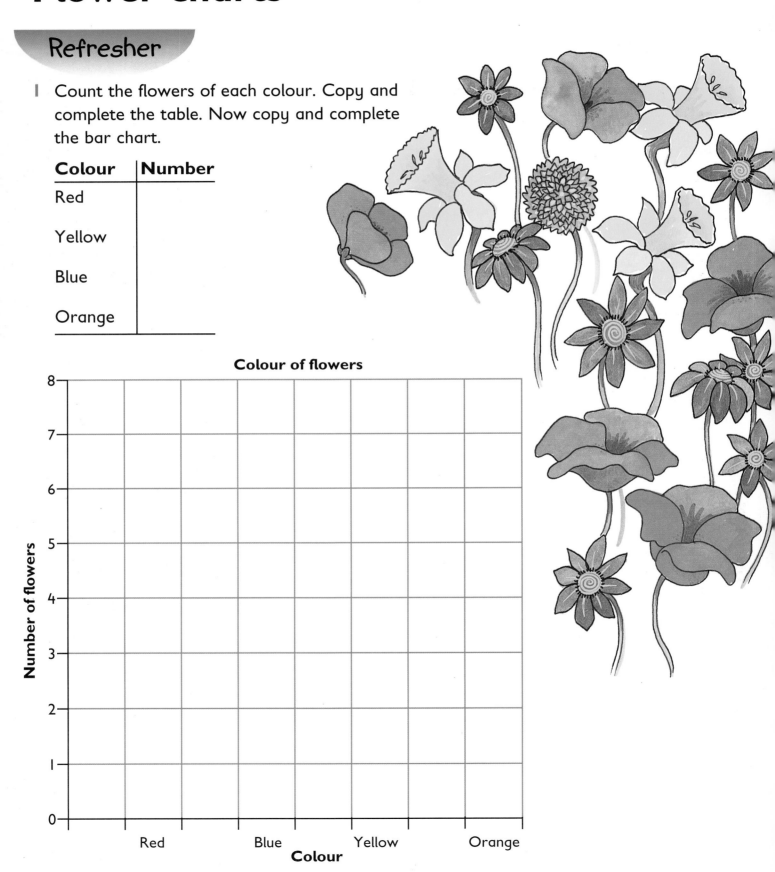

**Colour of flowers**

(bar chart with y-axis "Number of flowers" 0–8, x-axis "Colour": Red, Blue, Yellow, Orange)

## Practice

1 Count the cans of each type. Copy and complete the table. Now copy and complete the bar chart.

| Can | Number |
|---|---|
| Cola | |
| Lemonade | |
| Orange | |
| Cherry | |

**Cans of drink**

Number of cans

12 —
10 —
8 —
6 —
4 —
2 —
0 —

Cola   Lemonade   Orange   Cherry

**Drink**

● Solve a given problem by organising and interpreting numerical data in simple lists, tables and graphs, for example, bar charts

Sp 11, 3

# Down the road data

## Refresher

1  Make a tally mark to record all the things you can see in the street. Count the tally marks and write the totals.

|  | Tally | Total |
|---|---|---|
| Bus stops |  |  |
| Houses |  |  |
| Cars |  |  |
| Zebra crossings |  |  |
| People |  |  |

## Practice

1 Copy and complete the bar chart to record all the things
you can see in the street, then answer these questions.
  a What does the tallest bar show?
  b Are there more houses or cars?
  c How many bus stops and cars are there altogether?

**Things in my street**

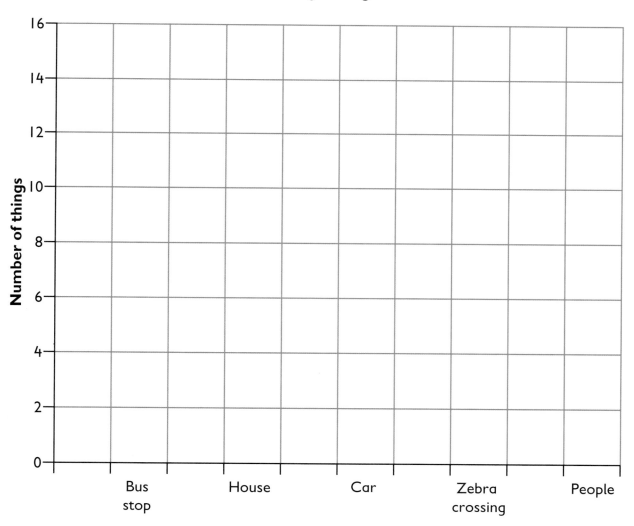

● Solve a given problem by organising and interpreting numerical data in simple lists, tables and graphs, for example, bar charts

Sp 11, 4

# Banana bar chart

## Refresher

1 Copy the table. Count the number of bananas each person ate. Write the totals in the table.

| Bananas | People |
|---------|--------|
| 3 | |
| 4 | |
| 5 | |
| 6 | |
| 7 | |

62

## Practice

1 Copy and complete the table on page 62. Draw a bar chart. Now answer these questions.
  a What was the largest number of bananas someone ate?
  b How many people ate five or six bananas?
  c How many people ate less than 4 bananas?

| Bananas | People |
|---------|--------|
| 3 | |
| 4 | |
| 5 | |
| 6 | |
| 7 | |

**Eating bananas**

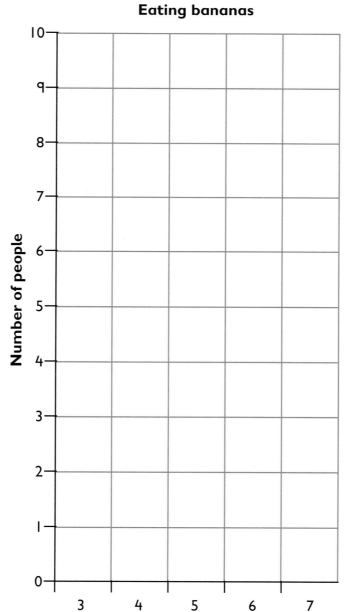

Number of people (vertical axis, 0 to 10)

Number of bananas (horizontal axis, 3 4 5 6 7)

# Spinner bar chart

## Refresher

Work in pairs.

1 Throw the die 50 times. Match the number to the animal. Make a tally mark for each animal. Count the tally marks and write the totals.

| Animal | Tally | Total |
|--------|-------|-------|
| dog | I | |
| | | |
| | | |
| | | |

## Practice

1 Match the number to the animal. Complete a bar chart to record the number of times each animal is thrown.

a What does the tallest bar show?

b Which animal did you get least?

c How many times did you get a dog?

d How many times did you get a cat?

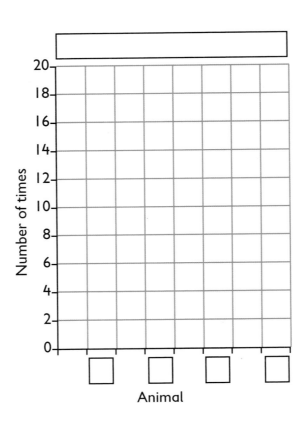

Number of times

Animal